the CHATEAU THOMAS table

pairing to perfection

Text copyright © 2008 by
Chateau Thomas Winery

Photography copyright © 2008 by Northstar Media, LLC d/b/a
Indianapolis dine magazine

Library of Congress Catalog-in-Publication Data available.

ISBN-13: 978-0-9820296-3-3

Manufactured in China

10 9 8 7 6 5 4 3 2 1

Northstar Media, LLC
120 East Vermont Street
Indianapolis, IN 46204

chateauthomas.com

northstarmediabooks.com

Forward

This cookbook was inspired during the planning of the celebration of the 25th anniversary of Chateau Thomas Winery, January 24, 2009. For the last 10 years, we have been serving food to patrons of our banquet facility. In lieu of those commercial recipes, we sought to include, instead, those masterpieces treasured by our owners, our staff, our friends, and our families. They have parted with some of their most personal and private recipes in order that this book could rise to the greatness emblematic of Chateau Thomas.

In the title pages of this publication, we have attempted to elaborate on the story of Chateau Thomas Winery in chapters devoted to the elements of its history that reveal and detail its soul. The first outlines the profile of the background and character of the man whose dreams were the genesis of this endeavor. The second chapter introduces his love and life partner whose input has been so instrumental in the creation of the wines and their names. In the third, Dr. Thomas' discovery and involvement in wine, his education, and his pursuit of his own stage of excellence is outlined. The fourth reveals the French influence that has tinted the image of Chateau Thomas as expressed in its experience, its name, and its wine style. In the final section, the development of the winery from its start to the present day multifaceted producer of Indiana's finest wines is recounted.

Correspondingly, the five chapters enumerate the five different elements of a menu and within, house the appropriate recipes for that portion of the meal. As with any cookbook, the recipes may not work for some, and may need modification, but all recipes have been tested in the kitchens of, and by the chefs of *Indianapolis dine* magazine to whom we are indebted for the production of this fine publication.

This book is dedicated to the loyal and devoted employees of Chateau Thomas Winery without whom, our success could not have been achieved.

"Therefore God gave thee of the dew of heaven, and the fatness of the earth, And plenty of corn and wine: "

Genesis 27:28, Old Testament

CHATEAU THOMAS WINERY

Choose one of these delicious varietals
from Dr. Charles Thomas' collection,
shown here from driest to sweetest.

VERDELHO

PINOT GRIGIO

CLASSIC CHARDONNAY

VERANDA ROSÉ

CABERNET SAUVIGNON

MERLOT

PINOT NOIR

CLASSIC MERLOT

DRY RIESLING

DRY GEWURTZTRAMINER

WHITE ZINFANDEL

MUSCAT CANELLI

RIESLING

CHARDONNAY CARNEROS

TANK-FERMENTED SAUVIGNON BLANC

UN-OAKED CHARDONNAY

VIOGNIER

SEMILLION

SYRAH

ZINFANDEL

TOSCA

TEMPRANILLO

SCOTT'S RED

VINTAGE PORT

LATE HARVEST VIOGNIER

LATE HARVEST RIESLING

CABERNET FRANC ICE WINE

VIDAL BLANC ICE WINE

Table of Contents

Appetizers and Cocktails

A Perfect Gin and Tonic 10
Artichoke Balls 11
Bacon-Wrapped Ginger Soy Scallops 13
Blue Tail Fly 14
Caviar and Radish Canapés 15
Caviar Supreme 16
Crab-Stuffed Mushrooms 17
Easiest Cheese Ball Ever 19
Goat Cheese Mushroom Tartlets 20
Strawberry Banana Smoothies 21

Salads and Soups

Asiago Cream Soup with Fideos 25
Easy Baked Applesauce 26
Gazpacho 27
Grilled Caesar Salad with Focaccia Croutons and Parmigiano Reggiano 28
Olive Eickhoff's Hot German Potato Salad 29
Southwestern Chili 31

Sides

Asian Glazed Carrots 34
Carrot Puff 35
Cheesy Potatoes 36
Cranberry Sauce 37
Crust-Topped Broccoli Cheese Bake 38
Herbed Turnips Dauphinois 39
Maple-Glazed Baby Carrots 40
Refrigerator Bran Muffins 41
Sizzling Italian Vegetables 43

Entrées

Asian-Style Flank Steak 47
Bacon Cheese Brats 48
Baguette Burger 50
Baked French Toast 51
Baked Spaghetti Squash 53
Barbecue Beef Brisket 55
Brined and Roasted Whole Turkey Basted with Citrus and Cranberry 56
Chicken Skewers with Peanut Sauce 57
Cordon Bleu 58
Deep-Fried Turkey 59
Ginger Scallops 61
My Mother's Meatloaf 62
Pleasing Wine Chicken 63
Glazed Pork Roast 64
Pork and Vegetable Chow Mein (Fried Noodles) 65
Quiche 67
Salt-Crusted Prime Rib Roast 69
Sausage Cheddar Fontina Strata 71
Sauteed Shrimp with Tomatoes, Garlic and Parsley 73
Smoked Cheddar-Stuffed Chicken 74
Steak Chinois 75
Tortilla Chili Pie 77

Desserts

Apple Raspberry Pan Dowdy 81
Espresso Brownies 83
Evangeline's Apple Cake 85
Freeze-Ahead Orange Soufflés 87
French Apple Pie 89
Italian Cheesecake 91
Molasses Cookies 92
Pear Tart 93

Eldest of three children, Charles Richard Thomas was born and raised by his hard-working parents, Gale and Margaret Thomas, and educated in the Indianapolis Public Schools. He was an avid swimmer as he and his siblings were regulars at the Riviera Club, where his uncle, Bill Lesch, was a lifeguard. He had *Indianapolis News* and *Indianapolis Star* newspaper delivery routes for six years. In high school, he spurned the schools in his northside district to attend Arsenal Technical High School, where he was able to major in science and journalism, and even take college-level courses, comparative anatomy and embryology. He was also the sports editor of the *Tech Cannon* newspaper.

He enrolled in Indiana University in Bloomington, Indiana, in the premedical program. He was a member of the Indiana University National Intercollegiate Billiards Team. Graduating from IU with a degree in anatomy and physiology, he was accepted into the Indiana University Medical School program, where he spent his first year in Bloomington and the last three in Indianapolis, graduating in 1958.

He interned at Methodist Hospital of Indiana for one year and then was accepted for a residency in OB-GYN at Methodist, where he realized his manual skills and ambidexterity were useful in surgery. During his residency, he received special training in vaginal surgery in Chicago, Illinois. Upon finishing his residency, he discovered there was only one OB-GYN on Indianapolis' southside, so he moved there.

His initial office location in 1962 was on U.S. 31, moving soon to the Turtle Creek Professional Building. In 1966, he took on a partner, then four years later added another. They incorporated as Southside OB-GYN and later expanded to include five physicians. Their offices were located by both St. Francis Hospital and Community South Hospital.

Dr. Thomas held many positions, both medical and civic, including President of the St. Francis Hospital Medical Staff, President of the Marion County Medical Society, and President of the Area V (Indiana) Professional Standards Review Organization.

He served as President of the Indianapolis Police Department Merit Board for seven years. He has received the Key to the City of Indianapolis twice, Sagamore of the Wabash, and Lt. Colonel in the Alabama Militia (by Governor George Wallace) for his support of The March of Dimes.

His 32 years of active practice yielded the delivery of 7,000 babies, expertise in complicated obstetrics, an accomplished vaginal surgeon and laparoscopist. He retired from medicine in 1995, having tired of government and insurance company intrusion into the practice of medicine.

In addition to working long, hard hours, he enjoyed bowling, swimming, tennis, basketball, scuba diving, playing pool, watching football and wood working. Fortunately, as a relatively young retiree, he had something else to do.

"Wine is at the head of all medicines; where wine is lacking, drugs are necessary." - *Babylonian Talmud*
"Wine...is a food" - *Sir Oliver Wendell Holmes*
"Wine is the most healthful and most hygienic of all beverages." - *Louis Pasteur*

Appetizers and Cocktails

A Perfect
Gin and Tonic

Adapted from a recipe by David Rosengarten, Food Author and Critic
Submitted by Dr. Charles Thomas, Chateau Thomas Winery Winemaker

Tonic water, as needed

1. At some time prior to preparing this drink, tonic water ice cubes should be made by freezing tonic water in an ice cube tray. Covered, they will remain fresh in the freezer for several weeks. Using these instead of regular ice cubes creates more flavor and less dilution as the ice melts.

COCKTAIL
4 tonic water ice cubes (more might be necessary to fill the glass)
3 ounces dry gin
4 ounces Schweppes Tonic Water, chilled
1 tablespoon freshly squeezed lime juice
1 lime slice, to garnish

1. Combine tonic water ice cubes, gin and tonic water in a cocktail glass.

2. Add lime juice on top of tonic water, but do not stir.

3. Garnish with a slice of lime.

SERVES 1

Artichoke Balls

By Glenda Steele, Chateau Thomas Winery Advertising Agency, Steele Communications

¼ cup butter
1 small onion, minced
1 15-ounce can artichoke hearts, drained and minced
1 clove garlic, minced
½ cup grated Parmesan cheese
½ teaspoon salt
½ cup toasted bread crumbs

1. Preheat oven to 300 degrees.

2. In a sauté pan, melt the butter and sauté the onion, artichoke, and garlic until onion is shiny. Remove from heat. Add cheese, salt and bread crumbs to the artichoke mixture.

3. Form mixture into 3-4 dozen bite-size balls. Bake in the 300-degree oven for 8-10 minutes.

YIELDS 3–4 DOZEN PIECES

WINE PAIRING | Chateau Thomas Winery Tank-Fermented Sauvignon Blanc

Bacon-Wrapped Ginger Soy Scallops

By Jill Thomas, Chateau Thomas Winery Corporate Secretary

¼ cup soy sauce
1 tablespoon packed brown sugar (or Splenda Brown Sugar
  Blend)
1½ teaspoons minced fresh ginger
6 very large Diver "dry"* sea scallops (8–10 ounces total)
1 8-ounce can sliced water chestnuts, drained
12 slices bacon, cut in half crosswise

1. Set the rack in the middle of the oven. Line the bottom of the broiler pan with aluminum foil, replace the perforated top part of the pan, and put the whole pan on the oven rack. Preheat oven to 450 degrees.

2. In a medium bowl, combine the soy sauce, brown sugar and ginger.

3. If the muscle tabs from the sides of the scallops are still attached, peel them off and discard. Cut each scallop into quarters. Marinate the scallop pieces in the soy mixture for 15 minutes. Reserve the marinade.

4. To assemble, stack 2 slices of water chestnuts in the center of a piece of bacon. Put a piece of scallop on top of the water chestnuts. Wrap each end of the bacon over the scallop and secure with a toothpick. Repeat with the remaining bacon, water chestnuts and scallops (you might not use all the water chestnuts).

5. Remove the broiler pan from the oven and quickly arrange the bacon-wrapped scallops on the hot pan so that an exposed side of each scallop faces up. Drizzle the scallops with the reserved marinade. Bake, turning the scallops over once after 10 minutes, until the bacon is browned around the edges and the scallops are cooked through (about 15 minutes total).

YIELDS 2 DOZEN HORS D'OEUVRES

*"Dry" scallops haven't been treated with any solution to maintain their shelf life, so they brown better, have a nicer texture and flavor, and tend to taste fresher than "wet" scallops.

WINE PAIRING | Chateau Thomas Winery Dry Gewürztraminer

Blue Tail Fly

Submitted by Dr. Charles Thomas, Chateau Thomas Winery Winemaker

2 ounces Crème de Cacao White liquor
3 ounces Blue Curacao liquor
2 ounces cream*

1. Add ingredients to a cocktail shaker filled halfway with shaved ice.

2. Shake vigorously.

3. Strain into a cocktail glass and serve.

SERVES 1

For a variation, a scoop of vanilla ice cream can be substituted for the cream. This requires mixing the cocktail in a blender.

An exotic dessert cocktail.

Caviar and Radish Canapés

By Dr. Charles Thomas, Chateau Thomas Winery Winemaker

24 slices white sandwich bread, very thinly sliced
1 large radish (or 1 daikon radish), 2 inches in diameter
¼ cup (6 ounces) cream cheese, at room temperature
2½ ounces prepared wasabi caviar*

1. Preheat the oven to 300 degrees.

2. Arrange the bread slices on two baking sheets. Place the bread slices in the oven to dry out and toast slightly, 5–7 minutes per side. Transfer to a wire rack to cool.

3. Slice the radish into ¹/₁₆-inch-thick slices. You can use a ¾-inch cookie cutter to cut the radish into uniform circles. Cover with damp paper towels and set aside.

4. Spread each bread slice with an even layer of cream cheese. Use a 2¼-inch cookie cutter to cut out 24 canapés. Working one at a time, spread ½ teaspoon of caviar on each canapé. Place a slice of radish on top of each canapé†. Serve immediately.

MAKES 24 CANAPÉS

Wasabi caviar is available at Saraga International Grocery, 317.388.9999.
†For the photograph, the chef added the radish first, then additional caviar.

WINE PAIRING | Chateau Thomas Winery Tank-Fermented

Caviar Supreme

By Dr. Charles Thomas, Chateau Thomas Winery Winemaker

1 package unflavored gelatin
1 cup cold water (or amount required on package instructions)

1. Soften gelatin in cold water and set cup in warm water to liquefy.

FIRST LAYER

4 hard-boiled eggs, finely chopped
½ cup Hellmann's brand mayonnaise
¼ cup dried parsley, finely chopped
2 green onions, finely chopped
¾ teaspoon salt
⅛ teaspoon Tabasco sauce

1. Combine all of the first layer ingredients. Mix thoroughly. Set aside.

SECOND LAYER

2 medium avocados, 1 pureed and 1 chopped
2 green onions, finely chopped
2 tablespoons lemon juice
2 tablespoons Hellmann's brand mayonnaise
½ teaspoon salt

1. Mix all second layer ingredients. Set aside.

THIRD LAYER

1 cup sour cream
¼ cup minced red or green onion

1. Mix third layer ingredients. Set aside.

2. Divide the gelatin into three equal parts, mixing one part in with each of the first three layer mixtures.

3. The day before you plan to serve the dish, grease the bottom and sides of a 8-inch springform pan or line the bottom and sides of a 1-quart soufflé dish with smooth foil, extending 4 inches above the rim. Spray lightly with cooking spray. Spread first layer into prepared dish. Smooth. Wipe side of dish clean above layer. Gently spread second layer mixture over the first layer. Smooth top and wipe foil clean above layer. Spread the third layer mixture over the second and smooth. Cover tightly with plastic wrap and refrigerate for 24 hours.

FOURTH LAYER

1 3½-ounce jar red or black caviar
Pumpernickel bread, sliced, to serve

1. To serve, lift the layers out of the dish by the foil "handles" and transfer with a large spatula onto a serving platter. Spread caviar over top. Serve with slices of pumpernickel bread.

YIELDS 4 CUPS

WINE PAIRING | Chateau Thomas Winery Chardonnay

An incredible taste and elegant appetizer.

Crab-Stuffed Mushrooms

By Jill Thomas, Chateau Thomas Winery Corporate Secretary

2 8-ounce packages fresh whole silver dollar-size mushrooms
½ stick butter
2 tablespoons minced garlic
1 8-ounce package cream cheese
1 8-ounce package imitation crabmeat
½ onion, diced
Salt, to taste
1 8-ounce package shredded mozzarella cheese

1. Clean and stem mushrooms. Preheat oven to 350 degrees.

2. In a saucepan over low heat, melt half stick of butter. Add 1 tablespoon garlic. Spread half of this mixture in the bottom of a greased sheet pan or casserole dish. Place mushrooms, caps down, in the dish. Spoon a small amount of the mixture into each mushroom cap, leaving room in each for additional stuffing. Bake at 350 degrees for 10-15 minutes, depending on their size.

3. In a separate mixing bowl, combine cream cheese, ¾ package crab, ½ diced onion, 1 tablespoon garlic and salt. Stuff mushrooms with mixture.

4. Bake at 350 degrees for 20 minutes. Remove from oven and top with mozzarella cheese. Put back in the oven until cheese melts.

SERVES 16

WINE PAIRING | Chateau Thomas Winery Verdelho

Easiest Cheese Ball Ever

By Lois Bailey, Chateau Thomas Winery Wine Club Member

2–3 8-ounce packages cream cheese (can substitute with
  light cream cheese)
1 package Buddig Corned Beef, chopped
4–6 whole scallions, chopped
1 teaspoon garlic powder
Crackers, to serve

1. Combine first four ingredients (cream cheese, corned beef,
scallions, garlic powder) thoroughly and shape into a ball.

2. Chill.

3. Serve with crackers.

WINE PAIRING | Chateau Thomas Winery Viognier

Goat Cheese Mushroom Tartlets

By Jill Thomas, Chateau Thomas Winery Corporate Secretary

3 tablespoons butter
8 ounces button mushrooms, cut into small pieces
1 large shallot, minced
⅛ teaspoon ground nutmeg
Salt and pepper, to taste
1 sheet frozen puff pastry (half of a 17.3-ounce package), thawed
1 large egg, beaten
3 ounces soft fresh goat cheese, at room temperature
2 tablespoons whipping cream
1 teaspoon minced fresh thyme

1. Melt 2 tablespoons butter in a heavy, large skillet over medium-high heat. Add mushrooms and sauté until soft, about 5 minutes. Add remaining 1 tablespoon butter and shallot to skillet. Sauté until shallot is soft, about 4 minutes. Add nutmeg. Season mushroom filling with salt and pepper, to taste, and cool.

2. Line soufflé cups with parchment paper.

3. Roll puff pastry out onto a lightly floured surface to a 12-by-15-inch rectangle. Cut out flat circles by using the bottom of a small juice glass. Press to seal edges Pierce pastry all over with a fork. Using a pastry brush, brush all sides of the pastry with the egg. These tartlet shells can be prepared 1 day ahead. Cover separately and refrigerate.

4. Preheat oven to 400 degrees. Bake tartlet shells on a greased or parchment paper-lined baking sheet until golden brown (about 12-15 minutes).

5. Maintain oven temperature. Spread cheese evenly over the bottoms of the tartlet shells. Top with mushrooms. Sprinkle with thyme, salt and pepper. Drizzle with cream. Bake until heated through, about 10 minutes. Serve hot.

MAKES 4 TARTLETS

WINE PAIRING | Chateau Thomas Winery Viognier

Strawberry Banana Smoothies

By Karen Thomas, Daughter of Chateau Thomas Winery Winemaker

1 ripe banana*
5-6 strawberries*, cleaned
1-2 cups ice
1 cup milk
Artificial sweetener, to taste

1. Place banana, strawberries and ice into the blender. Add milk. Blend until smooth and add sweetener, to taste. Serve and enjoy.

2. Place any leftovers in the freezer and drink within 24 hours.

SERVES 1

Other fruit and flavor options include peaches, apricots, blueberries and vanilla extract.

This is a wonderful treat suitable for diabetics. A perfect cool drink for those hot summer days.

The Love of His Life
CHATEAU THOMAS WINERY

One day in 1970, at St. Francis Hospital, he saw her! There, in the delivery suite, in a nurse's uniform, wearing a funny little hat from a nursing school in Dayton, Ohio (Miami Valley), was the love of his life. This little Buckeye, named Jill, also the eldest of three girls, was beautiful, witty, intelligent, an avid reader and gardener, a pianist, dancer and writer. Further, she was an outstanding cook with a broad repertoire of elegant dishes, many self-taught.

Charles and Jill were subsequently married in the chapel at Butler University on May 30, 1971. Their combined family of seven children was later enlarged to eight upon the arrival of Ryan Charles in 1974.

In 1979, tragedy struck when Jill was found to have an advanced case of non-Hodgkin's lymphoma. She soon became gravely ill. Just when the situation seemed hopeless, the grace of God guided the hand of Dr. Bill Dugan, an oncologist, to initiate a chemotherapeutic regimen that saved Jill's life. She remains today, Indiana's longest-living survivor of that cancer.

Just when things seemed back to normal, Jill's oldest son, Scott, developed Hodgkin's disease. Despite irradiation, chemotherapy and a bone marrow transplant, he succumbed to his disease in 1990. We have since dedicated a red wine to Scott in his memory, Scott's Red.

In the next few years, Jill attended several cooking classes to hone her skills and also volunteered as a counselor to patients in the Oncology Clinic at St. Francis. She now reads, gardens, quilts, takes care of the laundry, cleans house, counsels their children and has been active in their church. They are also members of a gourmet cooking group of eight couples that has been in existence since the early 1960s.

In the late 1990s, Jill began dancing with the Arthur Murray Dance Studio in Greenwood and quickly became one of their best dancers. She advanced to the gold level and earned five gold medals for her Arthur Murray studio in an international competition in Toronto. While proficient in most dances, Jill excelled in Latin dances. In 1999, a domestic accident caused an injury to her right knee, which interrupted her program, and after an otherwise remarkable recovery without surgery, Jill dances, but not competitively.

Jill is the vice president and corporate secretary of the winery. She remains an inspiration for Dr. Thomas with her wisdom, her love, her knowledge of cuisine, and her abilities as a wordsmith. When the winery needs a name or a solution to a problem, Jill's the one they call.

"A waltz and a glass of wine can invite an encore"
- Johann Strauss (1804-1849)

Salads
and Soups

Asiago Cream Soup with Fideos

By Dr. and Mrs. Charles Thomas, Chateau Thomas Winery Winemaker, Chateau Thomas Winery Corporate Secretary

½ cup unsalted butter
1 cup freshly grated Asiago cheese
3 egg yolks
1 cup heavy cream
1 cup Chateau Thomas Winery Chardonnay
4 cups chicken stock
4 ounces uncooked fideos*
Salt and freshly ground white pepper, to taste
Chopped fresh parsley or chives, to garnish

1. Cream the butter in a food processor. Add cheese and process for 2 additional minutes. Add the egg yolks one at a time, processing briefly after each addition. With the food processor running, add the cream. Scrape down the sides of the container and process again; set aside.

2. In a saucepan, bring the wine and chicken stock to a boil. Break the pasta into the saucepan. Cook for 8 minutes or until al dente.

3. Spoon some of the hot soup into the mixture in the food processor and process until smooth. Add to the saucepan. Bring to a simmer and season with salt and white pepper, to taste.

4. Ladle even portions into soup bowls and garnish with parsley or chives.

SERVES 6–8

Fideos are Spanish noodles. Check your local international market or Mexican section of your favorite local grocery.

WINE PAIRING │ Chateau Thomas Winery Chardonnay, Carneros

This is easy to make and very delicious.

Easy Baked Applesauce

By Linda Hastings, Daughter of Chateau Thomas Winery Winemaker

5 tablespoons water
¼ cup packed brown sugar (or Splenda Brown Sugar Blend)
2 tablespoons lemon juice
1 teaspoon ground cinnamon
4 pounds apples*, peeled, cored and sliced

1. Preheat oven to 375 degrees.

2. Combine all ingredients in a large Dutch oven; toss to coat. Cover and bake at 375 degrees for 1 hour and 15 minutes or until apples are tender, stirring once after 45 minutes.

SERVES 8 (½ CUP SERVINGS)

For best results, choose apples that break down easily when cooked, such as Gala, Pink Lady or Braeburn.

WINE PAIRING | Chateau Thomas Winery Dry Riesling

Gazpacho

By Gary Lane, Chateau Thomas Winery Graphic Artist

3 cups tomato juice
1 cup chicken broth
2 tablespoons olive oil
1 tablespoon fresh lemon juice
1 tablespoon hot sauce
1 cup bread crumbs
1 teaspoon sugar
1 teaspoon salt
½ teaspoon pepper
6 medium-size tomatoes, peeled, seeded and chopped
1 cucumber, peeled, seeded and chopped
1 stalk celery, chopped
1 large green pepper, diced
1 medium onion, finely chopped
2 garlic cloves, finely chopped
Croutons, to garnish (optional)
Sour cream, to garnish (optional)

1. In a large bowl, combine tomato juice, chicken broth, olive oil, lemon juice, hot sauce and bread crumbs. Stir in sugar, salt and pepper, to taste. Add all other vegetables and stir.

2. Take half the mixture and pour into a blender; blend until smooth. Combine back into one bowl, stir and chill.

3. Once cooled, serve garnished with croutons or sour cream.

SERVES 6

WINE PAIRING | Chateau Thomas Winery Dry Gewürztraminer

A delicious, spicy liquid salad.

Grilled Caesar Salad with Focaccia Croutons and Parmigiano Reggiano

By Dr. Charles Thomas, Chateau Thomas Winery Winemaker
(*Not Pictured*)

GARLIC OIL
¼ cup olive oil
2 whole cloves garlic, chopped

1. Combine the olive oil and garlic in a small pan. Slowly bring to a boil. Remove from heat. Let rest 30 minutes.

ROMAINE
6 tight hearts of romaine, core attached
3 tablespoons garlic oil (recipe above)
Salt and pepper, to taste

1. Rinse and dry romaine. Slice each heart in half and brush with garlic olive oil. Season with salt and pepper, to taste. Set aside for grilling.

FOCACCIA CROUTONS
1 pound focaccia bread
3 tablespoons garlic oil (recipe above)

1. Brush focaccia with garlic oil. Grill 30 seconds on each side. Cut into triangles 2 inches in diameter. Set aside for final presentation.

CAESAR DRESSING
½ teaspoon Tabasco sauce
1½ ounces grated Parmigiano Reggiano
1 tablespoon Worcestershire sauce
1 tablespoon white wine vinegar
1 tablespoon red wine vinegar
2 tablespoons balsamic vinegar
1 tablespoon black pepper
1 egg
4 cloves garlic, chopped
6 anchovies
½ lemon
Salt, to taste
1½ cups olive oil
1½ ounces shaved Parmigiano Reggiano

1. Combine all Caesar dressing ingredients, except olive oil and shaved Parmigiano Reggiano, in a food processor. Process until well blended. Slowly incorporate olive oil until emulsified. Season with salt and set aside for final preparation.

TO SERVE
1. Preheat grill to high heat. Grill the romaine approximately 5–10 seconds on each side.

2. On a 12-inch serving plate, place 3-4 croutons in the center. Atop croutons, place the grilled romaine. Spoon 2-4 tablespoons of the Caesar dressing over the romaine. Garnish with shaved Parmigiano Regianno and serve immediately.

SERVES 6

WINE PAIRINGS
Chateau Thomas Winery Sauvignon Blanc
Chateau Thomas Winery Verdelho

Olive Eickhoff's
Hot German Potato Salad

By Bill Dougherty, Chateau Thomas Winery Night Manager

10-12 potatoes
3-4 stalks celery
1 small onion
6 hard-boiled eggs, chopped
1½ cups sugar
1 teaspoon salt
1 teaspoon pepper
1 teaspoon celery seed
1 pound bacon
2 tablespoons flour
½-⅓ cup vinegar
¼-⅓ cup water

1. Boil potatoes until soft; peel and cube.

2. Dice celery and onion.

3. To a bowl with the potatoes, celery and onion, add eggs, sugar, salt, pepper and celery seed. Mix well.

4. Cut bacon into small pieces and place in a frying pan. Cook until crisp. Reduce heat to low and add flour, vinegar and water, stirring constantly. When thickened, remove from heat and pour over potato mixture.

SERVES 8

WINE PAIRING | Chateau Thomas Winery Chardonnay, Carneros

Southwestern Chili*

By Pete Gulesian, Chateau Thomas Winery Executive Chef

4 pounds ground sirloin
Salt and pepper, to taste
Chili powder, to taste
1 tablespoon olive oil
4-5 medium onions, diced
¾ bunch celery, chopped
3 cloves garlic, chopped
3-4 green bell peppers, diced
2 yellow bell peppers, diced
1 10-ounce can diced tomatoes
1 46-ounce can tomato juice
2 cups salsa of choice
2 40-ounce cans kidney beans
2 teaspoons ground cumin
2 pounds red potatoes, cubed
Shredded cheese of choice, to taste

1. In a large skillet, over medium heat, brown ground sirloin. Drain grease and season with salt, pepper and chili powder, to taste. Set aside.

2. To a large stockpot, add olive oil. Add the onions, celery, garlic and peppers and cook over medium heat until tender. Add the ground sirloin to the pot and adjust salt and pepper, to taste.

3. Add the diced tomatoes, tomato juice, salsa, kidney beans and cumin. Allow to cook slowly over medium heat. When fully cooked, add red skin potatoes. Allow chili to cook until potatoes are tender.

4. Serve topped with shredded cheese and your favorite chili accompaniments.

YIELDS APPROXIMATELY 4 GALLONS

This recipe makes a large amount, approximately 4 gallons. To feed your party, adjust the measurements as needed.

WINE PAIRING | Chateau Thomas Winery Sweet Aubergine

Proximate to the time of their marriage, Dr. and Mrs. Thomas began to drink wine with meals more often and their interest in wine accelerated. Dr. Thomas bought a kit from a Wine-Art store and began making wine. He joined a local club of amateur winemakers, The Society of Cellarmasters. As his wines improved, and he tried different varietals and sources, he began winning medals at amateur competitions. Sensing the need for better fruit for his wines, he began enticing area fruit merchants to bring grapes back from California for his wines. Chuckling, he remembers those trying days when all their children lined up in the basement to perform their respective duties in the bottling line!

In 1973, Dr. Thomas and two other Cellarmasters went to the Indiana State Fair Board and were granted permission to organize a wine competition which has now been renamed the Indy International Wine Competition, the second largest in the U.S. Dr. Thomas ran the judging for a few years, but then turned the reins over to others.

Percy Simmons, an Englishman with varied interests, was influential in Dr. Thomas' wine education. He hosted a regular course at Indiana University Purdue University Indianapolis called "Wine and its Uses." After attending the course in 1973, Dr. Thomas read voraciously about wine, and was elevated to senior instructor for the course from 1977-1993. During this time, he was introduced to many influential winemakers and wine promoters of the day whose counsel he has enjoyed for years since. After that course was cancelled, Dr. Thomas taught a similar class at Marian College for four years, then moved the classes to his winery.

In 1976, Dr. Thomas traveled to Napa Valley with National Wine and Spirits and again became more enchanted with the winemaking culture. He returned to California in 1978 and his friend, Marcia Mondavi (daughter of Robert Mondavi) arranged for him to obtain 25 pounds of cabernet sauvignon grapes, which he brought back on the airplane. In the years following, with his connections, he shipped fruit back to Indiana from good vineyards in Napa, California. That is, until the Med-fly infestation hit California and fresh fruit could not leave the state. He then contacted Peter Brehm, whose business was contracting good wine grapes, blast-freezing them, and then shipping them around the U.S. Over the next few years, this convenience and flexibility allowed Dr. Thomas to experiment in the production of several different varieties of grapes.

In 1983, Dr. Thomas made the decision to start a vinifera winery. When he informed Jill, she replied, "What took you so long?" He began to research the permits and preparations needed to start a winery, but felt he needed more education. He enrolled in The Napa Valley School of Cellaring and began classes, which were held every 3 weeks, starting in mid-1983. He would leave his medical office late in the morning on Fridays, fly to San Francisco, drive to Napa, and be in class by 1 p.m. Classes were virtually continuous until finished at noon on Sunday, whereupon he would fly home. Bruce Rector, a respected U.C Davis-educated enologist, the proprietor and lead instructor of the now-defunct school, is now retired from Glen Ellen Winery and remains a treasured friend and consultant. The school faculty consisted of many experts in enology, cooperage, chemistry and marketing. By the end of the year, Dr. Thomas had completed his certificate of winemaking core courses, and qualified to be a professional wine judge.

On January 19, 1984, Chateau Thomas Winery, BW-IN-15 was granted a federal wine license. Dr. Thomas intended that the winery would produce only vinifera (Old World grape) wines.

"Wine is the temperate, civilized, sacred, romantic mealtime beverage recommended in the Bible. It is a liquid food that has been part of civilization for 8000 years. Wine has been praised for centuries by statesmen, scholars, poets, and philosophers. It has been used as a religious sacrament, as the primary beverage of choice for food, and as a source of pleasure and diversion."
- Robert Mondavi (1913-2008)

Sides

This is a simple
but delicious dish.

Asian Glazed Carrots

By Linda Hastings, Daughter of Chateau Thomas Winery Winemaker

3 large carrots, peeled and sliced lengthwise
¼ cup water
2 tablespoons Kraft Asian Toasted Sesame Dressing
2 tablespoons orange juice

1. Cook carrots in water in a covered skillet over medium-high heat for 5-8 minutes or until carrots are crisp and tender.

2. Add remaining ingredients and toss to coat. Cook and stir 1-2 minutes or until heated through.

SERVES 2

WINE PAIRING | Chateau Thomas Winery Veranda Rosé

Carrot Puff*

By Dr. and Mrs. Charles Thomas, Chateau Thomas Winery Winemaker, Chateau Thomas Winery Corporate Secretary

1 pound carrots, peeled and cut into 1-inch pieces
½ cup (1 stick) butter, melted
3 eggs
1 cup granulated sugar or Splenda®
3 tablespoons all-purpose flour
1 teaspoon baking powder
1 teaspoon vanilla

1. Preheat oven to 350 degrees.

2. Grease a 8-inch square baking dish.

3. Place carrots in a medium-size saucepan and cover with salted water. Bring to a boil. Reduce heat and simmer, uncovered, for 20 minutes or until carrots are tender. Drain.

4. Place butter, eggs, sugar, flour, baking powder and vanilla in a blender. Add carrots in small batches and puree the mixture. Pour into prepared baking dish.

5. Bake at 350 degrees for 45 minutes or until firm. Let stand for 5 minutes before serving.

SERVES 6

This dish can be made a day ahead and refrigerated. Bring to room temperature before cooking.

WINE PAIRING | Best to match with the accompanying main course.

Cheesy Potatoes

By Karen Thomas, Daughter of Chateau Thomas Winery Winemaker

**2 30-ounce bags frozen hash browns (Ore-Ida brand works
well here)**
1 pound Velveeta, cubed
1 24-ounce jar mayonnaise

1. Preheat oven to 350 degrees.

2. Place hash browns in a 9-by-13-inch baking pan.

3. In a 2-quart saucepan, melt the cheese and mayonnaise
together, stirring constantly to prevent burning. When
cheese mixture is completely melted, pour over the top of the
potatoes and spread evenly. Place foil over the top.

4. Bake for 1 hour in the 350-degree oven. Remove foil and
continue to bake until the top is brown and bubbly, approximately
30 more minutes. Serve immediately and refrigerate any leftovers.

SERVES 20

WINE PAIRING | Chateau Thomas Winery Classic Chardonnay

This is a wonderful pitch-in
type dish. A true crowd-pleaser.

Cranberry Sauce

By Pete Gulesian, Chateau Thomas Winery Executive Chef

2 seedless oranges, peeled
9 cups fresh cranberries
1 cup Chateau Thomas Winery Fleur d'Peche
1 cup water
3 cups sugar
Cinnamon, to taste
Chateau Thomas Winery Sweet Sherry, to taste

1. Cut whole orange segments into small pieces. Place orange pieces and 3 cups cranberries into a food processor and mix until thoroughly combined.

2. To a large saucepan, add remaining cranberries, wine, water and sugar and simmer. Add processed cranberries and oranges to pan and continue to simmer. Cook until all berries are broken down and combined with sugar. Add cinnamon and sweet sherry, to taste. Refrigerate and serve.

SERVES 6

WINE PAIRING | Chateau Thomas Winery White Zinfandel

Crust-Topped Broccoli Cheese Bake

By Linda Hastings, Daughter of Chateau Thomas Winery Winemaker

½ cup (4 ounces) **Philadelphia Chive and Onion Cream Cheese spread**
1 10.75-ounce can **condensed cream of mushroom soup***
½ cup **water**
2 16-ounce packages **frozen broccoli florets, thawed and drained**
1 cup **shredded cheddar cheese**
1 **frozen puff pastry sheet, thawed**
1 **egg, lightly beaten**

1. Preheat oven to 400 degrees.

2. Mix cream cheese spread, soup and water until well blended. Stir in broccoli and cheddar cheese. Spoon the mixture into a greased 2½-3-quart rectangular or shallow oval baking dish.

3. On a lightly floured surface, roll out a sheet of puff pastry to fit the baking dish. Cover the top of the dish completely with the puff pastry sheet. Press pastry edges against the rim of the dish to seal. Brush the entire surface lightly with egg and pierce with a knife 5-6 times to vent.

4. Bake the mixture for 30 minutes or until heated through with the pastry puffed and golden brown.

SERVES 14

*You can substitute cream of chicken soup for cream of mushroom.

WINE PAIRING | Chateau Thomas Winery Sauvignon Blanc

Herbed Turnips Dauphinois

By Jill Thomas, Chateau Thomas Winery Corporate Secretary

1 large clove garlic
Butter, as needed
1 pound young turnips, peeled and thinly sliced
3 tablespoons all-purpose flour
¼ cup snipped fresh chives
1¼ cups whipping cream
½ teaspoon salt, plus more as needed
½ teaspoon freshly ground pepper
¼ teaspoon freshly grated nutmeg

1. Preheat oven to 350 degrees.

2. Rub a 7-by-10-inch porcelain or glass baking dish with garlic. Butter generously. Add a third of the turnips and sprinkle with 1 tablespoon flour, then a third of the chives. Add another layer by adding another third portion of the turnips, 1 tablespoon flour and third of the chives. Repeat a third time.

3. In a saucepan over medium-low heat, scald the cream with salt, pepper and nutmeg. Taste cream mixture and add more salt, if desired. Pour over turnips.

4. Cover with foil and bake in the 350-degree oven for 30 minutes. Remove foil and continue baking until turnips are tender, their tops are brown and the cream thickens (about 20 minutes). Serve hot.

SERVES 4

WINE PAIRING | Chateau Thomas Winery Chardonnay

Maple-Glazed Baby Carrots

By Linda Hastings, Daughter of Chateau Thomas Winery Winemaker

2 pounds baby carrots (regular will also work)
¼ cup reduced-fat Catalina salad dressing
¼ cup maple syrup
1 tablespoon butter
½ cup pecan pieces, toasted

1. Cook carrots covered in a saucepot of boiling water for 12-14 minutes or until tender. Drain; set aside.

2. In a separate saucepan, mix dressing and syrup. Cook over medium heat until mixture is bubbly, stirring occasionally. Add carrots and cook until glaze is thickened to desired consistency, stirring frequently. Add butter and stir until melted. Stir in pecans.

SERVES 10 ($^1/_2$ CUP SERVINGS)

WINE PAIRINGS
Chateau Thomas Winery Veranda Rosé
Chateau Thomas Winery Syrah (Shiraz)

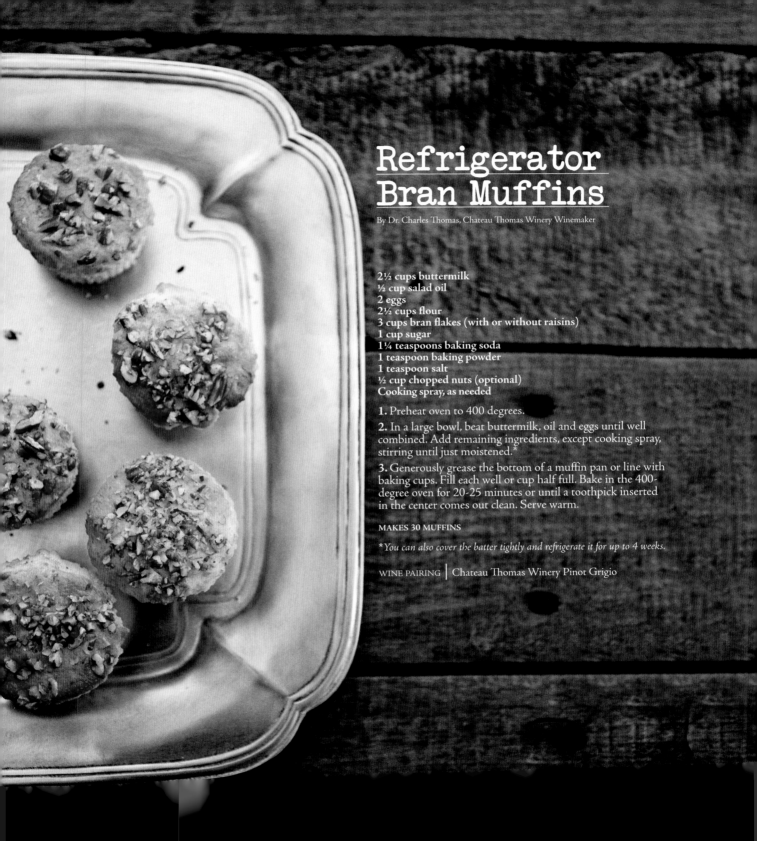

Refrigerator Bran Muffins

By Dr. Charles Thomas, Chateau Thomas Winery Winemaker

2½ cups buttermilk
½ cup salad oil
2 eggs
2½ cups flour
3 cups bran flakes (with or without raisins)
1 cup sugar
1¼ teaspoons baking soda
1 teaspoon baking powder
1 teaspoon salt
½ cup chopped nuts (optional)
Cooking spray, as needed

1. Preheat oven to 400 degrees.

2. In a large bowl, beat buttermilk, oil and eggs until well combined. Add remaining ingredients, except cooking spray, stirring until just moistened.*

3. Generously grease the bottom of a muffin pan or line with baking cups. Fill each well or cup half full. Bake in the 400-degree oven for 20-25 minutes or until a toothpick inserted in the center comes out clean. Serve warm.

MAKES 30 MUFFINS

*You can also cover the batter tightly and refrigerate it for up to 4 weeks.

WINE PAIRING | Chateau Thomas Winery Pinot Grigio

Sizzling Italian Vegetables

By Linda Hastings, Daughter of Chateau Thomas Winery Winemaker

1 zucchini, coarsely chopped*
1 tomato, chopped
2 tablespoons balsamic vinaigrette dressing
2 slices cooked bacon, chopped
¼ cup shredded low-moisture, part-skim mozzarella cheese†

1. In a skillet over medium-high heat, cook zucchini, tomato, dressing and bacon for 6-8 minutes or until zucchini is crisp and tender and mixture is heated through, stirring occasionally.

2. Sprinkle mixture with cheese.

SERVES 4

*You can substitute 1½ cups sliced fresh mushrooms or coarsely chopped fresh green beans for the zucchini.
†You can substitute ¼ cup grated fresh Parmesan cheese for the mozzarella.

WINE PAIRING | Chateau Thomas Winery Pinot Grigio

The French Influence
CHATEAU THOMAS WINERY

In the mid-1970s, while teaching and reading about wine, the French influence was undeniable, and Dr. Thomas was enthralled with French techniques of winemaking, including extended barrel aging, blending and long-aging potential. California wines were just gaining respect at that time, having just bested French wines in the legendary tasting of 1976. During that time, Dr. Thomas occasioned on a cellar of a deceased acquaintance that was for sale. That launched his fascination with older wines. He began to buy wines at auction and collected with a vengeance. He eventually assembled the world's largest collection of 1928 French Bordeaux wines, which were later recognized at a seven-day charity event in Puerto Rico, with the famous Michael Broadbent and a host of wine experts, including Dr. Thomas, conducting the tasting of those 40 different wines.

Dr. Thomas also collected many other French wines which he favored. He has a large collection of Chateau Gruaud Larose, his favorite Bordeaux, dating from 1869.

In 1975, Percy Simmons inducted Dr. Thomas into the prestigious Confrerie des Chevaliers du Tastevin, recognized as the original French (Burgundy) wine and food organization with chapters all over the world. Dr. Thomas was later elected Grand Senechal of the local chapter and Grand Officier in the Grand Council Amerique. He later was inducted into several other wine and food organizations, including The International Wine and Food Society, La Confrerie de la Chaine des Rotisseurs (established in 1258), L'Ordre Mondial des Gourmets Gustaters, La Confrerie des Gouste Vin de Normandie, Les Amis du Vin, and La Confrerie de St. Etienne d'Alsace. With these groups, Dr. and Mrs. Thomas have visited France about nine times, to study both the winemaking methods and the cuisine of France. They have many close friends in France, including Comte Alexandre Lur-Saluces of Chateau d'Yquem, Jean-Michel Cazes of Chateau Lynch-Bages, and Jean-Charles Thomas of Domaine Charles Thomas in Burgundy.

The Thomas' English influence ranged from Michael Broadbent to the legendary Harry Waugh, the best wine taster in history. He published 17 wine books before he died at age 96. Harry was a dear friend to both Jill and Charles. He would make a yearly wine tasting tour of the U. S., then publish the results in a book. He visited Indianapolis regularly, holding wine dinners and tastings. He always stayed for a few days with the couple (Jill even did his laundry). He and Jill are mentioned with their pictures in two of his books. They treasure his memory!

Dr. and Mrs. Thomas have also enjoyed their varied and elegant culinary experiences right here in Indianapolis. The Tastevin has also staged some wonderful dinners that have inspired some of the menus included in this tome. Instead of the usual 6-minute American lunch, they fondly remember the 3½-hour, six-course lunches enjoyed in Normandy and Burgundy, where conversation is as important as the food.

The sum total of all their Francophilic experiences has molded the approach Dr. Thomas takes in his winemaking. He feels wine should be a beverage that has a life. Even though the wine world is being led to the drink-now persuasion, Dr. Thomas feels allowing wine to mature and develop in the barrel, to undergo judicious fining, and benefit from the art of imaginative blending is what produces fine, elegant, and durable wines that can be cellared for years or decades. He feels that California grapes are superior because of the abundant sunlight and dry climate. Therefore, he uses those West Coast grapes to produce Old World-style wines in Indiana. He has won over 500 international awards by the end of 2008.

It is no accident that the winery was named Chateau Thomas Winery.

"I drink Champagne when I'm happy and when I'm sad. Sometimes I drink it when I'm alone. When I have company, I consider it obligatory. I trifle with it when I'm not hungry and drink it when I am. Otherwise I never touch it - unless I'm thirsty."
- Lily Bollinger, French Vintner (1899-1977)

Entrées

Asian-Style Flank Steak

By Linda Hastings, Daughter of Chateau Thomas Winery Winemaker

½ cup dry sherry
⅓ cup soy sauce
2 tablespoons ketchup
2 cloves garlic, minced
1½ tablespoons minced, peeled fresh ginger
1 tablespoon Asian sesame oil
1 1½-1¾-pound flank steak

1. Whisk all ingredients, except meat, in a 12-by-9-by-2-inch baking pan. Add steak; turn to coat. Let marinate at room temperature for 2 hours, turning occasionally.

2. Preheat broiler. Transfer steak to a broiler pan. Drain marinade from dish into a medium saucepan; boil for 3 minutes.

3. Broil steak until cooked to desired doneness, about 4 minutes per side for medium-rare. Transfer steak to a platter and let stand for 5 minutes. Cut crosswise into thin slices and serve, passing cooked marinade as the sauce.

SERVES 4

WINE PAIRING | Chateau Thomas Winery Syrah (Shiraz)

Bacon Cheese Brats

By William Walker, Father-in-law of Chateau Thomas Winery Winemaker

TOPPING SAUCE
⅓ cup mayonnaise
2 tablespoons whole-grain mustard
2 tablespoons honey
1 teaspoon apple cider vinegar
¼ teaspoon dry mustard
3 cups coleslaw cabbage mix
2 tablespoons chopped fresh parsley
¼ cup minced scallions
¼ teaspoon cayenne pepper
Salt, to taste

1. In a medium mixing bowl, whisk mayonnaise, whole-grain mustard, honey, vinegar and dry mustard to combine. Add cabbage, parsley, scallions, cayenne pepper and salt; toss to coat, then drain so that the slaw is not too runny. Chill mixture.

BRATS

8 strips thinly-sliced bacon
8 precooked all-turkey or all-beef brats
8 Coney buns
8 slices American cheese, cut in half

1. Preheat grill to medium-high heat. Preheat broiler to high heat with the rack 6 inches from the fire. Partially cook bacon in the microwave or on the grill.

2. Wrap bacon around brats in a barber pole manner, one strip per brat. Secure with toothpicks if necessary.

3. Grill brats, turning every 2 minutes, until bacon is crisp, about 5-7 minutes.

4. Place buns facedown on the broiler until partially toasted. Turn buns over and place ½ slice of cheese on each side of the bun and bake until cheese melts, about 2 minutes.

TO SERVE

1. Remove toothpicks and place brats on buns. Top with slaw and enjoy.

MAKES 8 BRATS

WINE PAIRING | Chateau Thomas Winery Dry Riesling

Baguette Burger*

By Jill Thomas, Chateau Thomas Winery Corporate Secretary

1 12-inch-long French baguette
Butter, as needed
1 pound ground chuck†
1 egg
2 tablespoons bread crumbs
2 tablespoons water
¼ cup minced onion
1½ teaspoons McCormick's Hamburger Seasoning
1-2 teaspoons Worcestershire sauce
Salt and pepper, to taste
Cheese of choice, as needed (optional)

1. Preheat oven to 350 degrees.

2. Divide baguette lengthwise and crosswise into 4 equal pieces. Butter the baguettes and toast in the 350-degree oven until crisp, about 6-7 minutes.

3. Blend the ground chuck and remaining ingredients, except cheese, in a bowl. Divide into four equal portions. Mound the chuck mixture evenly on top of each baguette.

4. Bake in the 350-degree oven for about 20-25 minutes. If desired, add your favorite cheese to the top of each baguette during the final 2 minutes of baking. Serve immediately.

SERVES 4

*This is an open-faced sandwich. The top bun shown in this photo was used simply for presentation.
†Regular hamburger is too greasy for this recipe. Ground round is too dry.

WINE PAIRING | Chateau Thomas Winery Classic Merlot

Baked French Toast*

By Jill Thomas, Chateau Thomas Winery Corporate Secretary

6-9 slices French bread, cut on an angle to ½-1-inch width
1 3-ounce package cream cheese, softened
1½ teaspoons cinnamon, plus extra to taste
3 eggs, beaten
1 cup milk
1 tablespoon sugar or Splenda
1 teaspoon vanilla extract
½ cup butter, melted
Maple syrup, to serve

1. Preheat oven to 380 degrees.

2. Apply a thin coat of softened cream cheese to both sides of each bread slice. Place the bread in a 9-by-13-inch baking dish. Sprinkle with cinnamon.

3. Mix together the eggs, milk, sugar, 1½ teaspoons cinnamon, vanilla and melted butter. Pour the egg mixture over the bread and let stand for 30-60 minutes.

4. Bake in the 380-degree oven for 15-20 minutes. Do not overbake! Serve immediately with warm maple syrup.

SERVES 6–9

*This recipe can be partially prepared a day ahead by spreading the bread with cream cheese and mixing together the eggs, milk, sugar, cinnamon and vanilla. The following morning, add the melted butter to the egg mixture, pour over the bread, let stand 20-30 minutes and then bake.

WINE PAIRING | Chateau Thomas Winery Chardonnay, Carneros

This is a great summer dish that is
low in calories and easy to fix.

Baked Spaghetti Squash*

By Karen Thomas, Daughter of Chateau Thomas Winery Winemaker

1 spaghetti squash
Salt and pepper, to taste (optional)
Butter, margarine or olive oil, to taste (optional)

1. Preheat oven to 425 degrees.

2. Carefully cut squash in half lengthwise. Remove seeds. Place cut sides of squash down on a cookie sheet or in an oven-safe pan. Bake in the 425-degree oven for at least 45 minutes. The squash is ready when a fork is easily inserted in the vegetable through the outer skin. Remove from oven.

3. Turn halves over so the cut side is facing up. Using a fork, begin scraping the "meat" of the squash away from the shell. The squash will appear string-like, similar to spaghetti. Transfer from the shell to the serving dish. Depending on your preferences, you can season with salt and pepper, butter, margarine or olive oil for added flavor.

SERVES 6

For a special treat, scrape the squash into strings but leave in the shell. Season, to taste. Top the vegetable with shredded cheese and/or spaghetti sauce. Place back in the oven until the cheese is melted or sauce is heated. Create your own tasty dish and enjoy!

WINE PAIRING | Chateau Thomas Winery Tank-Fermented Sauvignon Blanc

This recipe has been a family favorite for 25 years. It is complicated in that there are three parts: A rub for the meat, a mop sauce for cooking and a barbecue sauce for serving. Yum!

54

Barbecue Beef Brisket

By Dr. and Mrs. Charles Thomas, Chateau Thomas Winery Winemaker, Chateau Thomas Winery Corporate Secretary

RUB
⅓ cup salt
⅓ cup chili powder
2½ tablespoons MSG or Accent
1½ tablespoons black pepper
1 tablespoon garlic powder

1. Blend all rub ingredients. This can be stored indefinitely.

MOP SAUCE
5 ounces beef consommé
5 ounces water
3 ounces Worcestershire sauce
3 ounces cider vinegar
3 ounces vegetable oil
¾ teaspoon dry mustard
½ teaspoon chili powder
½ teaspoon Tabasco sauce
1 small bay leaf
¼ teaspoon paprika

1. Make the mop sauce several hours ahead to allow the flavors to marry. Simply combine the mop sauce ingredients and set aside or refrigerate.

BARBECUE SAUCE*
2 cups ketchup
1½ cups apple cider vinegar
½ cup Worcestershire sauce
1½ cups packed brown sugar
3 tablespoons dry mustard
6 tablespoons chili powder
1½ teaspoons ground ginger
6 tablespoons butter
6 thin slices lemon

1. Combine all barbecue sauce ingredients in a saucepan. Bring to a boil and simmer for 5 minutes. Cool, remove lemon slices, pour into a large jar, cover and refrigerate to use as needed.

This yields about 1¼ quarts of sauce. It can be used for BBQ chicken or ribs as well.

To Serve

1 5-6-pound brisket

1. Preheat charcoal grill to medium heat. If using a gas grill, heat to medium-high heat.*

2. Massage the rub mixture into the brisket and place meat on the grill 8-10 inches over an even bed of glowing coals. Add new coals as old ones burn down and, if possible, a handful of hickory chips to the coals or smoking pan. If the grill has a kettle top, cover the meat tightly. If not, cover loosely with a sheet of heavy foil.

3. Grill for 1 hour; brush with the mop sauce. Cook 4 hours longer (5 hours total), brushing with the mop sauce every hour.

4. Remove the brisket from the heat, thinly slice and serve with barbecue sauce.

SERVES 11

This recipe can be prepared in the oven as well. Place brisket in an uncovered pan in a 250-degree oven and roast using the same method and timing as above.

WINE PAIRING | Chateau Thomas Winery Zinfandel

Brined and Roasted Whole Turkey Basted with Citrus and Cranberry

By Pete Gulesian, Chateau Thomas Winery Executive Chef

1 cup cranberry juice
1 cup Chateau Thomas Winery Muscat Canelli
Juice of 2 oranges
2 cups Morton Coarse Kosher Salt
1 cup sugar
2-3 gallons cool water
1 12-15-pound fresh whole bone-in, skin-on turkey, rinsed and patted dry
½ teaspoon ground black pepper mixed with 3 tablespoons softened butter
3 tablespoons melted butter
1 cup white wine, chicken broth or water

1. Make the basting liquid by combining the cranberry juice, wine and orange juice.

2. To brine, in a stockpot, dissolve salt and sugar in cool water. Submerge turkey in brine, cover and refrigerate for 4-5 hours. Remove the turkey. Rinse inside and out under cool running water for several minutes to remove all traces of salt. Pat dry with paper towels.

3. To roast, preheat oven to 450 degrees. Place turkey on rack in roasting pan. Rub black pepper/butter mixture under the skin. Brush melted butter over skin.

4. Pour wine, broth or water into the bottom of a pan. Roast turkey at 450 degrees for 25 minutes, baste, and rotate the pan. Continue roasting until skin turns golden brown (an additional 25 minutes). Baste again.

5. Lower the temperature to 325 degrees and continue to roast, basting and rotating the pan once about halfway through cooking, until the internal temperature reaches 170 degrees in the turkey breast and 180 degrees in the turkey thigh. Remove the turkey from the oven. Let stand 20 minutes before carving.

SERVES 24

WINE PAIRING | Chateau Thomas Winery Merlot

Chicken Skewers with Peanut Sauce

By Linda Hastings, Daughter of Chateau Thomas Winery Winemaker

¼ cup Catalina salad dressing
3 tablespoons creamy peanut butter
1 tablespoon soy sauce
1 pound boneless, skinless chicken breasts, cut lengthwise into slices
2 tablespoons dry roasted peanuts, chopped
¼ cup chopped green onions

1. Mix the salad dressing, peanut butter and soy sauce in a large bowl until well blended. Add chicken; toss to coat. Cover and refrigerate for 10 minutes to marinate.

2. Preheat broiler. Remove chicken from marinade and discard marinade. Thread chicken evenly onto 8 soaked wooden or metal skewers. Place on the oven rack in a broiler pan.

3. Broil 4-5 inches from heat for 4 minutes on each side or until cooked through. Serve sprinkled with peanuts and onions.*

SERVES 4 (2 SKEWERS EACH)

*Get creative with the leftovers. Remove chicken from skewers, chop and add to a mixture of lettuce, mixed greens and shredded carrots and toss with Kraft Asian Toasted Sesame salad dressing.

WINE PAIRINGS
Chateau Thomas Winery Veranda Rosé
Chateau Thomas Winery Syrah (Shiraz)

Cordon Bleu

By Glenda Steele, Chateau Thomas Winery Advertising Agency, Steele Communications

8 4-ounce slices milk-fed veal
4 slices Swiss cheese
4 slices ham, thinly sliced
Salt and pepper, to taste
Flour, as needed
2 eggs, whipped
1 cup bread crumbs
Oil, for frying
Fresh lemon, to garnish
Fresh parsley, to garnish

1. Preheat oven to 350 degrees.

2. Layout 1 slice veal. On top of that slice, add 1 slice Swiss cheese, 1 slice ham and top with another slice of veal. Fold together and press lightly. Season with salt and pepper, to taste.

3. Roll veal wrap in flour, whipped eggs and bread crumbs. Press together gently.

4. In a large skillet, heat oil to medium-high heat. Fry veal portions in a skillet until golden brown. Turn only once. Finish in the 350-degree oven for approximately 15 minutes.

5. Serve garnished with lemon and parsley. Bon appetite!

SERVES 4

WINE PAIRING | Chateau Thomas Winery Tempranillo

When I was handling public relations for a large ad agency, we represented a restaurant whose chef was named "Indianapolis' best". He appeared on TV and cooked this dish. It's an easy recipe and it will impress your dinner guests.

Deep-Fried Turkey

By Dr. Charles Thomas, Chateau Thomas Winery Winemaker

1 whole turkey (up to 22 pounds)
¾ cup Private Harvest Pure Grapeseed Oil*
6 tablespoons Robert Rothschild Pesto Bread Dipping
  Spices*
2 tablespoons (1 ounce) Chateau Thomas Merlot
Approximately 4 gallons peanut oil†

1. Rinse and dry the turkey, removing the neck and giblets from the body cavity.

2. Mix the grapeseed oil and the spices together; then add the wine and mix thoroughly to make a marinade.

3. Massage 2 tablespoons of the bread dipping spices all over and under the turkey skin.

4. Using a long-needled injector, inject the marinade into all of the meaty portions of the bird. Place in the refrigerator overnight.

5. When you're ready to make the turkey, prepare the peanut oil in the deep fryer or large pot according to the manufacturer's specifications and to the desired temperature. For your safety, prepare the cooking apparatus outside.

6. Place the turkey on a cooking platform; place an internal thermometer into the breast without touching any bone. Slowly lower the bird into the hot oil. Stand back at least 2 feet and wear protective clothing because of the hot oil!

7. Cook the bird approximately 3 minutes per pound, to an internal temperature of 168 degrees.

8. Allow the turkey to rest for 20 minutes before serving.

SERVES 10 (DEPENDING ON THE SIZE OF THE TURKEY)

*Available at Chateau Thomas Winery in Plainfield.

† A helpful trick to estimate the amount of oil needed, is to place the raw turkey into the cooking pot before any treatment. Add water until it is about 1-2 inches above the bird. Then, measure the water. That will be the amount of oil you will need. Note that oil can be reused and, in fact, browns the turkey better the second time.

WINE PAIRING | Chateau Thomas Winery Merlot

Ginger Scallops

By Dr. Charles Thomas, Chateau Thomas Winery Winemaker

2 tablespoons finely chopped green onion
2 tablespoons butter
1 large carrot, julienned
2 tablespoons finely chopped fresh ginger
½ cup Chateau Thomas Winery Chardonnay
½ cup whipping cream
Salt and freshly ground pepper, to taste
1¼ pounds medium-size scallops

1. In a skillet, saute the green onion in 1 tablespoon butter. Add the carrot and cook for 30 seconds. Add ginger; then stir in the wine. When thoroughly heated, add the cream, salt and pepper, and cook over high heat until the sauce is reduced by half.

2. Add scallops and cook 1 minute.

3. Turn off heat. Stir in remaining 1 tablespoon butter and serve.

SERVES 2–4

WINE PAIRING | Chateau Thomas Winery Muscat Canelli

[The Muscat Canelli] will really bring out the sweetness in the scallops. The ginger in the recipe matches very well with the aromas of the selection.
– Dr. Thomas

My Mother's Meatloaf

By Kathy Funke, Wife of Chateau Thomas Winery Director of Sales

1½ pounds lean ground beef
¾ cup chopped onion
¼ cup medium-dice red or yellow bell pepper
¾ cup old-fashioned oats, uncooked
½ cup ketchup
1 egg, slightly beaten
1 tablespoon Worcestershire sauce
2 cloves garlic, minced
½ teaspoon salt
¼ teaspoon black pepper

1. Preheat oven to 350 degrees.

2. Combine all ingredients in a large bowl and mix lightly. Shape meatloaf mixture into a 10-by-6-inch loaf and place on rack of broiler pan.

3. Bake 50-55 minutes for medium doneness, or until the loaf is no longer pink in the center and juices show no pink color. Let stand 5 minutes before slicing.

4. Cover and refrigerate leftovers promptly and use within 2 days, or wrap airtight and freeze up to 3 months.

SERVES 6

WINE PAIRING | Chateau Thomas Winery Scott's Red

Pleasing Wine Chicken

By Linda Hastings, Daughter of Chateau Thomas Winery Winemaker

1 8-ounce container sour cream
½ cup Chateau Thomas Winery Pinot Noir
1 can cream of mushroom soup
2 tablespoons minced garlic
1 teaspoon salt
1 teaspoon pepper
½ cup flour plus ¼ cup water mixture (thickener)
6 large boneless, skinless chicken breasts

1. Preheat oven to 350 degrees.

2. In a mixing bowl, combine the sour cream, chardonnay, cream of mushroom soup, garlic, salt, pepper and flour.

3. Place chicken breasts in a greased baking dish and pour mixture over meat. Cover with aluminum foil and bake at 350 degrees for 1 hour. You can also make this dish in a Crock-Pot.

SERVES 6

WINE PAIRING | Chateau Thomas Winery Pinot Noir

Glazed Pork Roast

By Linda Hastings, Daughter of Chateau Thomas Winery Winemaker

1 pork loin or pork roast
½ cup water
½ cup apricot preserves
2 tablespoons brown sugar
1 tablespoon soy sauce

1. Preheat oven to 325 degrees.

2. Place pork loin or pork roast in a roasting bag. Set aside.

3. In a small bowl, combine water, apricot preserves, brown sugar and soy sauce. Spread evenly over the pork. Fasten roasting bag.

4. Bake pork in the 325-degree oven until it reaches an internal temperature of 160 degrees.

SERVES 10

WINE PAIRING | Chateau Thomas Winery Semillon

Pork and Vegetable Chow Mein (Fried Noodles)

Recipe by Jill Thomas, Chateau Thomas Winery Corporate Secretary
(Not pictured)

If you plan on preparing this recipe, Chinese cooking requires several principles that must be strictly adhered to: **1.** *Advance preparation of all ingredients.* **2.** *A very hot wok (400-450 degrees). An electric wok will not be hot enough. Do not use a Teflon wok as the high heat will ruin it.* **3.** *Oil should be heated almost to the smoky stage.* **4.** *Stir constantly while stir-frying.*

MARINADE
½ tablespoon cornstarch
1 tablespoon soy sauce
1 tablespoon white wine
½ teaspoon sugar

CHOW MEIN
½ pound partially frozen pork loin (partially frozen is easier to slice)
½ pound bean sprouts
½ cup water chestnuts, sliced
¼ pound snow peas
2 green onions, sliced
10 ounces vegetable or peanut oil

SAUCE
1½ tablespoons oyster sauce
½ teaspoon sugar
½ teaspoon salt
1 tablespoon cornstarch
¾ cup chicken broth

1. Prepare the marinade by combining the cornstarch, soy sauce, white wine and sugar.

2. Slice the pork loin very thinly and submerge in the marinade for 30 minutes.

3. Slice the chow mein vegetables (bean sprouts, water chestnuts, snow peas, onions) and set aside.

4. Combine the sauce ingredients in a bowl and set aside.

5. Heat 3 tablespoons of oil in a wok. Stir-fry the pork for 3 minutes or until cooked through and remove meat from wok.

6. Drain all of the remaining oil and wipe out the wok.

7. Heat 2 tablespoons of oil. Stir-fry all of the vegetables, adding the snow peas last, over high heat for about 3 minutes.

8. Add the sauce and cooked pork. Mix well and fry for about 2 minutes. Serve over rice and, if desired, La Choy brand crispy rice noodles on top.

SERVES 4

WINE PAIRINGS
Chateau Thomas Winery Pinot Noir
Chateau Thomas Winery Sauvignon Blanc

We have many out-of-town, and sometimes, surprise overnight guests. I usually have all the ingredients for this quick and easy dish that can be served any time of the day.

Quiche

By Glenda Steele, Chateau Thomas Winery Advertising Agency, Steele Communications

6 eggs
1½ cups milk
1 teaspoon salt
¼ teaspoon poultry seasoning (if using chicken)
9-inch deep-dish pie shell
1 cup shredded cheese of choice*
½ pound ground sausage or chicken*
Fresh fruit, to serve

1. Preheat oven to 375 degrees.

2. Using a handheld mixer, beat the eggs, milk and seasonings.

3. Line a 9-inch pie pan with the pastry shell. Sprinkle cheese and sausage/chicken into the bottom of the shell. Pour egg mixture over that. Cover edges loosely with foil, or use a pie ring.

4. Bake at 375 degrees for 40 minutes and serve with fresh fruit.

SERVES 8

You can substitute any ingredients you want in place of cheese, sausage or chicken. Some suggestions include ham, bacon, turkey, Swiss cheese, spinach, broccoli, onions and green peppers.

WINE PAIRING | Chateau Thomas Winery Un-Oaked Chardonnay, Carneros

This recipe is a modification of the original used for years at the famous Red Key restaurant in Redkey, Indiana. This preparation results in a juicy roast because the juices have been sealed in by the salt. There is also a flavorful salty taste at the periphery of the meat.

Salt-Crusted Prime Rib Roast

By Dr. Charles Thomas, Chateau Thomas Winery Winemaker

4 cups rock salt (kosher or coarse-ground varieties)
¾ cup coarsely ground black pepper
1 cup olive oil
Approximately 2 cups flour
1 15-16-pound prime rib roast (6 or more bones)

1. In a large bowl or food processor, combine the rock salt, pepper and the oil and then add the flour until it achieves the consistency of a very thick paste.

2. Place the roast on a cutting board, bone side up. Rub the bone side of the meat with 2 tablespoons of the salt paste. Turn the roast over onto a large piece of aluminum foil, exposing the meaty side. Pack the paste all over the meaty and fatty surfaces so that it adheres and forms a casing over the meat. It will probably be necessary to press the paste onto the meat in order to adhere. It may also be necessary to use the foil to aid in keeping the paste over the vertical sides. Let the roast sit for 1 hour.

3. Preheat the oven to 450 degrees.

4. Roast the rib roast for 1 hour, or until the crust is slightly darkened. Lower the temperature to 300 degrees and roast for another 2 hours and 15 minutes, or until a meat thermometer inserted into the meat, but not touching bone, registers 135 degrees for medium-rare. Transfer the roast back onto the cutting board to rest for 30 minutes, but, remember, it is still cooking!

5. Carefully lift the crust off the meat and place the crust in a bowl. It is often difficult to break the crust and a hammer may be necessary (it may make a mess). It is more of a display if the crust can be removed with the bones from the piece of meat intact. Try to insert a knife under the bones and lift them off if you can. You will likely have to brush off some pieces of salt. Carve the roast into desired slices and serve. Some of the crumbled salt crust can be used as a condiment.

SERVES 16

WINE PAIRINGS
Chateau Thomas Winery Cabernet Sauvignon
Chateau Thomas Winery Merlot

Sausage Cheddar Fontina Strata

By Dr. Charles Thomas, Chateau Thomas Winery Winemaker

12 ounces sweet Italian sausage links, casing removed
6 large eggs
2 cups reduced-fat (2 percent) milk
¼ teaspoon salt
¼ teaspoon coarsely ground black pepper
8 slices firm white sandwich bread, toasted
4 ounces (1 cup) shredded cheddar cheese
3 ounces (3/4 cup) shredded fontina cheese
¼ cup loosely packed fresh parsley leaves, chopped

1. Grease a 8-by-8-inch glass or 1½-quart ceramic shallow baking dish.

2. In a separate 12-inch nonstick skillet, cook sausage over medium heat for 13-14 minutes or until browned, stirring occasionally and breaking up sausage with the side of your spoon. Transfer to paper towels to drain.

3. Meanwhile, in a medium bowl, using a wire whisk, beat eggs, milk, salt and black pepper until well blended.

4. Arrange 4 slices of bread in the bottom of a greased baking dish, cutting slices if necessary. Sprinkle with cheddar cheese and sausage. Cover with the remaining slices of bread. Slowly pour egg mixture over bread; press bread down to help it absorb the egg mixture. Top with fontina cheese. Let strata stand at room temperature for 15 minutes, or cover and refrigerate overnight.

5. Preheat oven to 350 degrees. Bake strata for 40 minutes or until puffed and golden, or until the tip of a knife inserted in the center comes out clean. (If strata is refrigerated overnight, uncover and bake 50 minutes.) Let stand at least 10 minutes to set custard before serving. Sprinkle with chopped parsley to serve.

6 ENTRÉE-SIZE SERVINGS

WINE PAIRINGS
Chateau Thomas Winery Muscat Canelli
Chateau Thomas Winery Classic Chardonnay

Sauteed Shrimp with Tomatoes, Garlic and Parsley

By Pete Gulesian, Chateau Thomas Winery Executive Chef

2 ounces olive oil
2 ounces unsalted butter
2½ pounds 35-count shrimp
4 ounces diced tomatoes
2½ teaspoons finely chopped garlic
¼ cup chopped fresh parsley
2 teaspoons diced shallots
⅛ cup Chateau Thomas Winery Muscat Canelli
Salt and pepper, to taste
Handful shredded Parmesan cheese
1 pound cooked fettuccine

1. Heat oil and butter in a large sauté pan over medium heat.

2. Dry each shrimp with a paper towel. Carefully add shrimp to sauté pan and allow them to cook for 1-2 minutes, until they are almost fully cooked. Add tomatoes, garlic, parsley, shallots and wine. Allow mixture to cook for approximately 2 minutes or until shrimp is fully cooked and liquid begins to simmer.

3. Reduce heat, add salt and pepper, to taste. Toss in Parmesan cheese and serve over a bowl of warm fettuccine.

SERVES 10 (4 OUNCE SERVINGS)

WINE PAIRING | Chateau Thomas Winery Sauvignon Blanc

Smoked Cheddar–Stuffed Chicken

By Linda Hastings, Daughter of Chateau Thomas Winery Winemaker

½ cup coarsely grated smoked cheddar cheese
1 tablespoon plus ¼ cup pure maple syrup
1 tablespoon cream cheese, at room temperature
2 teaspoons chopped fresh sage
4 boneless chicken breast halves, skin and tenderloin
   attached*
¼ cup Scotch whisky
2 tablespoons golden brown sugar, packed
2 tablespoons unsalted butter
Nonstick vegetable oil spray, as needed

1. In a small mixing bowl, blend cheddar cheese, 1 tablespoon maple syrup, cream cheese and sage. Keep handy.

2. Place 1 chicken breast, skin side down, on a work surface. Using a small, sharp knife, cut a 1½-by-2-inch horizontal pocket in the chicken. Pack in ¼ of the cheese stuffing. Press tenderloin into pocket opening to seal in stuffing. Repeat with remaining chicken breast and stuffing. Arrange chicken on a small baking sheet.

3. Combine ¼ cup maple syrup, whisky, brown sugar and butter in a small saucepan. Whisk over medium heat until sauce comes to a simmer and is well blended.†

4. Spray grill rack with nonstick spray and heat barbecue grill to medium-high heat. Reheat basting sauce; transfer half to a bowl and reserve. Set pan with remaining sauce at the edge of the grill to keep warm. Grill chicken, skin side down, until golden (about 3 minutes). Turn chicken over, repositioning over medium to medium-low heat. Grill until cooked through, turning occasionally (about 8 minutes). Baste the meat with sauce during the last 5 minutes. Transfer the chicken to a platter. Serve with remaining sauce on the side.

SERVES 4

*If you cannot find boneless chicken breasts with skin and tenderloin attached, use boneless, skinless chicken breasts. Soak some toothpicks in water and use them to close the opening and help hold in the stuffing.

†The chicken and basting sauce can be made a day ahead. Cover separately and refrigerate.

WINE PAIRING | Chateau Thomas Winery Sauvignon Blanc

This is a simple recipe and most of the ingredients you will have on hand. It's the perfect entree to serve to company.

Steak Chinois

By Linda Hastings, Daughter of Chateau Thomas Winery Winemaker

7 tablespoons canola oil, divided
¼ cup plus 1 tablespoon tamari sauce or soy sauce
3 tablespoons plus 1 teaspoon finely grated, peeled
  fresh ginger
2 cloves garlic, chopped
1½ pounds flank steak, uncooked
1¼ cups whipping cream
4 tablespoons sliced green onions, divided
Pepper, to taste
Rice or noodles, cooked, to serve

1. Mix 6 tablespoons oil, ¼ cup tamari/soy sauce, 3 tablespoons ginger and garlic in a greased 13-by-9-by-2-inch glass dish. Add steak, turning to coat. Cover and refrigerate overnight.

2. Remove steak from marinade and pat dry. Heat 1 tablespoon oil in a large skillet over high heat. Add steak; cook until browned, about 4 minutes per side for medium-rare. Transfer the steak to a platter.

3. Reduce heat to medium-high. Add cream and 2 tablespoons green onions to skillet. Bring to a boil, scraping up browned bits. Add 1 tablespoon tamari/soy sauce and 1 teaspoon ginger. Boil to sauce consistency, about 3 minutes. Season sauce with pepper.

4. Cut steak across grain on diagonal into ¼-inch-thick slices. Divide steak among 4 plates. Drizzle with sauce and sprinkle with 2 tablespoons green onions. Serve over noodles or rice.

SERVES 6

WINE PAIRING | Chateau Thomas Winery Barbera

We visited a dear friend in Oklahoma many years ago and she served this authentic Mexican dish. It came in handy when she had to feed her hungry ranchers and I make it for family gatherings.

Tortilla Chili Pie

By Glenda Steele, Chateau Thomas Winery Advertising Agency, Steele Communications

Flour tortillas, as needed
1½ pounds lean ground beef
1 medium onion, chopped
1 large clove garlic, minced
2 teaspoons chili powder
1 teaspoon cumin
2 8-ounce or 1 16-ounce jar tomato sauce
1 12-ounce can whole kernel corn, drained
1 20-ounce can chili beans
1 7.75-ounce can ripe olives, sliced
1 16-ounce (large) bag corn tortilla chips
2 cups shredded cheddar cheese

1. Preheat oven to 350 degrees.

2. Line a 9-by-12-inch baking dish with tortillas, overlapping as necessary.

3. In a sauté pan, brown and crumble beef until cooked through. Drain off all but 3 tablespoons of fat. Add onion, garlic, chili powder and cumin. Cook until onion is limp. Stir in tomato sauce, corn, chili beans and olives. Pour into tortilla-lined pan and arrange tortilla chips on top of mixture.

4. Bake, uncovered, at 350 degrees for 15-20 minutes. Sprinkle with grated cheese and continue baking for 15 minutes. Serve with extra tortilla chips.

SERVES 12

WINE PAIRING | Chateau Thomas Winery Tosca

The Chateau Blossoms

CHATEAU THOMAS WINERY

In 1984, the original winery was located on the southside of Indianapolis in an office/warehouse suite of 1,200 square feet. When Dr. Thomas released his first vintage, the first restaurant to place his wines on their wine list was his friend, Dieter Puska, owner of the famous Glass Chimney Restaurant. Other restaurants followed and the Chateau Thomas brand was on its way.

Shortly after opening, Dr. Thomas' eldest son, Steven, came to work for him in the winery to help make the wine while Dr. Thomas was practicing medicine. As business increased, Dr. Thomas purchased a building on Troy Avenue across from the Pleasant Run Golf Course. This building provided more production space and a better retail location. The next move was to lease space in the first and later second floor of a charming, vine-covered building at 501 Madison Avenue, just south of Union Station. In 1995, the search was on again for a new location.

At the same time, space was leased in Nashville, Indiana, a small tourist/retail hamlet to sell wine. His son also departed to establish his own winery. The Nashville facility has moved to a second location, Coachlight Square, and now has a wine bar with live music on weekends.

In researching traffic patterns, it was decided that Exit 66 on Interstate 70 was the preferred location in the Cambridge Square Park Development. Located on just over one acre of land on a roundabout only 200 feet from I-70, he erected a 10,000-square-foot, two-story building with a tasting room, offices, production space, locker space for private wine collections, and a banquet room and kitchen. Two additions have been added since for more storage and more public and banquet space. In 2008, an adjacent building on one acre of land was purchased to provide additional parking and outdoor food and wine service. His Music on the Veranda Friday night music events are well-known in the Indianapolis area.

During the last 25 years, Dr. Thomas has steadily improved the quality and quantity of his wines. He steadily established sources for good grapes for his wines. "You can make bad wine from good grapes, but you can't make good wine from bad grapes!" he says. His relationships are enduring and solid, such as his history of yearly purchase of chardonnay and pinot noir grapes from the finest producer in North America, Sangiacomo Vineyards, since 1986.

Contracted grapes are picked, chilled, and then shipped in refrigerated trucks to Plainfield in 3 days or less. The winemaking process begins at the winery. This scenario is not unique, nor original, but Dr. Thomas was perhaps the first to produce wine by this process from California grapes in Indiana, doing so as early as 1979. His wines have been served in the Indiana Governor's Mansion, to the President and Vice-President of the United States, and were the only wines served to 130 attendees of a banquet in an 18th century Castle in France.

Dr. Thomas has also endeavored to remain in touch with the latest developments in wine production, chemistry, and technology. With expanded gift shoppe space showcasing over 4,000 items, the tasting room is the most elegant in Indiana. Likewise, the lobby has displays of winemaking relics and history, displays of grape origins, and displays of some of the medals they have garnered. The winery is located amongst 15 hotels with more than 1,000 rooms within walking distance. With plans to establish, in 2009, The Hendricks County Convention and Visitors Center 300 feet away, The Indianapolis International Airport two miles away, and expansion of the Exit 66 interchange, Chateau Thomas Winery is in the center of it all.

"No nation is drunken where wine is cheap; and none sober where the dearness of wine substitutes ardent spirits as the common beverage. It is in truth the only antidote to the bane of whiskey."
- Thomas Jefferson (1743-1826)

Desserts

Apple Raspberry Pan Dowdy

By Jill Thomas, Chateau Thomas Winery Corporate Secretary

2 20-ounce cans apple pie filling
1½ cups frozen raspberries
¼ teaspoon cinnamon
10 ounces canned flaky biscuits
1 tablespoon margarine or butter, melted
2 teaspoons sugar*

1. Preheat oven to 400 degrees.

2. In a 12-by-8-inch, 2-quart baking dish, mix together the apple pie filling, raspberries, and cinnamon.

3. Bake at 400 degrees for 10 minutes, or until fruit is hot.

4. Separate biscuits and arrange over fruit. Brush with butter and sprinkle with sugar. Return to the oven and bake for an additional 15-20 minutes, or until it reaches a deep golden color on top.

SERVES 10

*3 teaspoons of erythritol (Zerose®) can be substituted with no calories or aftertaste. This ingredient is readily available on the Internet or at many local health food stores.

WINE PAIRINGS
Chateau Thomas Winery Riesling
Chateau Thomas Winery Vidal Blanc Ice Wine
Chateau Thomas Winery Cabernet Franc Ice Wine

Espresso Brownies

By Jill Thomas, Chateau Thomas Winery Corporate Secretary

Vegetable cooking spray, as needed
⅓ cup plus 2 tablespoons water
⅓ cup vegetable oil
2 large eggs
4 tablespoons espresso powder
1 box Betty Crocker® Brownie Supreme mix
¾ cup semisweet chocolate chips
1 teaspoon vanilla extract
½ cup powdered sugar
½ cup Splenda Sugar Blend
1 teaspoon milk
1 tablespoon unsalted butter, at room temperature

1. Preheat oven to 350 degrees.

2. Spray a 9-by-13-inch baking pan with vegetable cooking spray. Whisk ⅓ cup of water, oil, eggs, and 2 tablespoons espresso powder in a large bowl until blended. Add the brownie mix and stir until well blended. Stir in the chocolate chips. Transfer the batter to the prepared baking pan.

3. Bake until a toothpick inserted in the center of the brownies comes out with a few moist crumbles attached, about 35 minutes. Cool completely.

4. Meanwhile, in a medium bowl, dissolve the remaining 2 teaspoons espresso powder in the remaining 2 tablespoons water. Whisk in the vanilla. Add the powdered sugar, Splenda, milk and butter and whisk until smooth. Pour the glaze over the cooled brownies. Cut into squares and serve.

MAKES 36 SMALL BROWNIES

WINE PAIRING | Chateau Thomas Winery Vintage Port

Evangeline's Apple Cake

By Sheila Kavanaugh, General Manager Chateau Thomas Winery

CAKE
1 cup sugar
1 teaspoon baking soda
2 cups sliced Granny Smith apples
1 egg
1½ cups flour
1½ teaspoons cinnamon
1 cup raisins

1. Preheat oven to 375 degrees.

2. In a large bowl, sprinkle sugar and baking soda over apples and let stand until juicy. Add all other cake ingredients and mix well.

3. Pour batter into a 9-by-13-inch greased baking pan and bake at 375 degrees for 40 minutes.

TOPPING
½ cup brown sugar
½ cup sugar
1 cup water
1 stick butter
1 teaspoon vanilla extract
2 tablespoons flour

1. While cake is baking, in a saucepan, combine brown sugar, sugar, water, butter, vanilla and flour. Heat over medium heat until thickened.

2. Allow the cake to cool for 15 minutes and then pour topping over cake to serve.

SERVES 12

WINE PAIRING | Chateau Thomas Winery Riesling

Freeze-Ahead Orange Soufflés

By Dr. and Mrs. Charles Thomas, Chateau Thomas Winery Winemaker, Chateau Thomas Winery Corporate Secretary

SOUFFLÉ

¼ cup butter
½ cup sifted flour
¼ teaspoon salt
1 cup milk
½ cup sugar
3 eggs, separated
⅓ cup orange juice
1 teaspoon lemon juice
4 teaspoons grated orange rind
1 teaspoon grated lemon rind
3 tablespoons orange-flavored liqueur (Cointreau or Grand Marnier)

1. Melt butter in a heavy saucepan over moderate heat. Stir in flour and salt. Add milk and ¼ cup sugar; cook, stirring constantly, until thick. Remove from heat.

2. Beat egg yolks, orange juice, lemon juice, rinds and liqueur; beat well. Beat the flour mixture into the egg yolk mixture.

3. In a separate bowl, beat egg whites until they hold soft peaks. Add remaining ¼ cup sugar, 1 tablespoon at a time, and beat until whites are stiff and glossy. Fold egg yolk mixture into whites. Pour into 6-ounce custard or soufflé cups. Wrap in plastic film, seal and freeze.

4. To serve, preheat oven to approximately 350 degrees. Remove wrapping and set dishes in a pan of hot water. Bake in the 350-degree oven for about 1 hour or until puffed, brown and firm. Serve immediately with Fluffy Orange Sauce (recipe at right).

SERVES 6–8

FLUFFY ORANGE SAUCE

2 eggs, separated
½ cup sugar
½ cup orange juice
¼ cup lemon juice
1½ teaspoons grated orange rind
½ teaspoon grated lemon rind
⅛ teaspoon salt

1. Using a handheld mixer, beat egg yolks and sugar until light and lemon colored. Stir in fruit juices, rinds and salt.

2. Pour the mixture into a saucepan and cook over low heat, stirring constantly, until thickened.

3. Beat egg whites until they hold soft peaks; fold cooked egg yolk mixture into egg whites. Serve with Freeze-Ahead Orange Soufflés.

YIELDS ABOUT 1½ CUPS

WINE PAIRING | Chateau Thomas Winery Vidal Blanc Ice Wine

This was my grandmother's apple pie recipe and a family favorite. It's a great dessert especially when topped off with some ice cream.

French Apple Pie

By Linda Hastings, Daughter of Chateau Thomas Winery Winemaker

PIE PASTRY
1 cup flour
⅓ cup plus 1 tablespoon shortening
½ teaspoon salt
2½ tablespoons cold water

1. Preheat oven to 450 degrees.

2. Mix together flour, shortening and salt using a pastry blender. Sprinkle water over the mix and blend into the mixture.

3. Gather dough together and press into a ball shape. Roll out and place in a greased pie pan. Bake in the 450-degree oven for 10 minutes. Remove pie crust and reduce oven heat to 350 degrees.

PIE FILLING
¾ cup sugar
1½ teaspoons cinnamon
6-7 cups Granny Smith apples, peeled, cored and sliced
Butter, as needed

1. Mix sugar and cinnamon together. Sprinkle ⅓ of cinnamon mixture into the bottom of the crust. Arrange half of the apples in the pan. Sprinkle top of the apples with half of the remaining cinnamon mixture. Dot lightly with butter. Place half of the remaining apples in the pie. Top with remaining cinnamon mixture and dot with butter. Put the remainder of the apples on the pie. Cover top of the apples with the crumb topping (recipe below).

CRUMB TOPPING
¾ cup butter
¾ cup brown sugar
1½ cups flour

1. Using a handheld mixer, cream butter and brown sugar. When mixture is smooth, cut in flour. Mixture should have varying sizes of lumps. Put crumb topping over top layer of apples. (You may need to lightly press crumbs into place.)

2. Place pie in the 350-degree oven and bake 1 hour.

SERVES 8

WINE PAIRING | Chateau Thomas Winery Late Harvest Riesling

Italian Cheesecake

By Dr. and Mrs. Charles Thomas, Chateau Thomas Winery Winemaker, Chateau Thomas Winery Corporate Secretary

CRUST
5 tablespoons sugar
2 cups graham cracker crumbs
7 tablespoons butter, melted

1. Thoroughly blend sugar and crumbs. Incorporate butter.

2. Firmly press the crust mixture against the bottom and sides of a 10-inch springform pan.

CAKE
2 8-ounce packages cream cheese, softened
8 ounces sour cream
1 cup sugar
1 13-ounce can evaporated milk
2 tablespoons flour
5 egg yolks, at room temperature
1 teaspoon vanilla extract
5 egg whites, beaten stiff but not dry
½ teaspoon cinnamon

1. Preheat oven to 375 degrees.

2. Using a handheld mixer, beat the cream cheese until smooth. Add sour cream and sugar; beat well. Add evaporated milk, flour, egg yolks and vanilla; beat well. Fold in egg whites.

3. Pour batter into crust-lined pan and sprinkle with cinnamon.

4. Bake at 375 degrees for 30 minutes, then 350 degrees for 45 minutes. Turn oven off and leave cake in oven for 30 minutes with door closed. Open oven and allow cake to remain in open oven for another 30 minutes. This helps prevent cracking of the top surface. Refrigerate.

SERVES 16

WINE PAIRING | Chateau Thomas Winery Late Harvest Viognier

Molasses Cookies

By Jill Thomas, Chateau Thomas Winery Corporate Secretary

½ cup butter
½ cup shortening
1½ cups sugar, plus extra for coating cookies
½ cup molasses
2 eggs, lightly beaten
4 cups flour
½ teaspoon salt
2¼ teaspoons baking soda
2¼ teaspoons ginger
1½ teaspoons cloves
1½ teaspoons cinnamon

1. Preheat oven to 350 degrees.

2. In a large mixing bowl, cream butter, shortening and sugar until light colored and fluffy. Beat in molasses and eggs; set mixture aside.

3. In another bowl, combine flour, salt, baking soda, ginger, cloves and cinnamon. Mix well. Gradually mix flour mixture into creamed ingredients until dough is blended and smooth. Roll dough into 1½-inch balls. Dip in sugar.

4. Bake at 350 degrees for 11 minutes.

WINE PAIRING | Chateau Thomas Winery Muscat Canelli

I won a first place ribbon at the Indiana State Fair with this cookie recipe!

Pear Tart

By Dr. Charles Thomas, Chateau Thomas Winery Winemaker

1 cup plus 3 tablespoons sugar
6 tablespoons flour
3 eggs
1½ sticks butter
2 Bartlett pears, peeled, cored and quartered lengthwise
1 10-inch pie shell, unbaked
Powdered sugar, to taste

1. Preheat oven to 375 degrees.

2. Combine granulated sugar, flour and eggs in a large bowl and whisk until smooth.

3. In a medium skillet over high heat, melt the butter until foamy and golden brown. Slowly whisk melted butter into sugar mixture.

4. Cut pears crosswise into ⅛-inch-thick slices. Arrange pears in a flower petal pattern in the crust. Pour melted butter mixture, slowly, over pears.

5. Bake at 375 degrees until crust and filling are brown, 45-60 minutes. Serve warm or at room temperature. Just before serving, sprinkle top with powdered sugar, if desired.

SERVES 8

WINE PAIRING | Chateau Thomas Winery Late Harvest Viognier

Index

A

A Perfect Gin and Tonic, 10

APPETIZERS + COCKTAILS
A Perfect Gin and Tonic, **10**
Artichoke Balls, **11**
Bacon-Wrapped Ginger Soy Scallops, **13**
Blue Tail Fly, **14**
Caviar and Radish Canapés, **15**
Caviar Supreme, **16**
Crab-Stuffed Mushrooms, **17**
Easiest Cheese Ball Ever, **19**
Goat Cheese Mushroom Tartlets, **20**
Strawberry Banana Smoothies, **21**

Apple Raspberry Pan Dowdy, **81**
Artichoke Balls, **11**
Asiago Cream Soup with Fideos, **25**
Asian Glazed Carrots, **34**
Asian-Style Flank Steak, **47**

B

Bacon Cheese Brats, **48**
Bacon-Wrapped Ginger Soy Scallops, **13**
Baguette Burger, **50**
Baked French Toast, **51**
Baked Spaghetti Squash, **53**
Barbecue Beef Brisket, **55**
Blue Tail Fly, **14**
Brined and Roasted Whole Turkey Basted with Citrus and Cranberry, **56**

C

Carrot Puff, **35**
Caviar and Radish Canapés, **15**
Caviar Supreme, **16**
Cheesy Potatoes, **36**
Chicken Skewers with Peanut Sauce, **57**
Cordon Bleu, **58**
Crab-Stuffed Mushrooms, **17**
Cranberry Sauce, **37**
Crust-Topped Broccoli Cheese Bake, **38**

D

Deep-Fried Turkey, **59**

DESSERTS
Apple Raspberry Pan Dowdy, **81**
Espresso Brownies, **83**
Evangeline's Apple Cake, **85**
Freeze-Ahead Orange Soufflés, **87**
French Apple Pie, **89**
Italian Cheesecake, **91**
Molasses Cookies, **92**
Pear Tart, **93**

E

Easiest Cheese Ball Ever, **19**
Easy Baked Applesauce, **26**

ENTRÉES
Asian-Style Flank Steak, **47**
Bacon Cheese Brats, **48**
Baguette Burger, **50**
Baked French Toast, **51**
Baked Spaghetti Squash, **52**
Barbecue Beef Brisket, **55**
Brined and Roasted Whole Turkey Basted with Citrus and Cranberry, **56**
Chicken Skewers with Peanut Sauce, **57**
Cordon Bleu, **58**
Deep-Fried Turkey, **59**
Ginger Scallops, **61**
My Mother's Meatloaf, **62**
Pleasing Wine Chicken, **63**
Glazed Pork Roast, **64**
Pork and Vegetable Chow Mein (Fried Noodles), **65**
Quiche, **67**
Salt-Crusted Prime Rib Roast, **69**
Sausage Cheddar Fontina Strata, **71**
Sauteed Shrimp with Tomatoes, Garlic and Parsley, **73**
Smoked Cheddar-Stuffed Chicken, **74**
Steak Chinois, **75**
Tortilla Chili Pie, **77**

Espresso Brownies, **83**
Evangeline's Apple Cake, **85**

F

Freeze-Ahead Orange Soufflés, **87**
French Apple Pie, **89**

G
Gazpacho, **27**
Ginger Scallops, **61**
Glazed Pork Roast, **64**
Goat Cheese Mushroom Tartlets, **20**
Grilled Caesar Salad with Focaccia Croutons and Parmigiano Reggiano, **28**

H
Herbed Turnips Dauphinois, **39**

I
Italian Cheesecake, **91**

M
Maple-Glazed Baby Carrots, **40**
Molasses Cookies, **92**
My Mother's Meatloaf, **62**

O
Olive Eickhoff's Hot German Potato Salad, **29**

P
Pear Tart, **93**
Pleasing Wine Chicken, **63**
Pork and Vegetable Chow Mein (Fried Noodles), **65**

Q
Quiche, **67**

R
Refrigerator Bran Muffins, **41**

S
SALADS + SOUPS
  Asiago Cream Soup with Fideos, **25**
  Easy Baked Applesauce, **26**
  Gazpacho, **27**
  Grilled Caesar Salad with Focaccia Croutons and Parmigiano Reggiano, **28**
  Olive Eickhoff's Hot German Potato Salad, **29**
  Southwestern Chili, **31**

Salt-Crusted Prime Rib Roast, **69**
Sausage Cheddar Fontina Strata, **71**
Sauteed Shrimp with Tomatoes, Garlic and Parsley, **73**

SIDES
  Asian Glazed Carrots, **34**
  Carrot Puff, **35**
  Cheesy Potatoes, **36**
  Cranberry Sauce, **37**
  Crust-Topped Broccoli Cheese Bake, **38**
  Herbed Turnips Dauphinois, **39**
  Maple-Glazed Baby Carrots, **40**
  Refrigerator Bran Muffins, **41**
  Sizzling Italian Vegetables, **43**

Sizzling Italian Vegetables, **43**
Smoked Cheddar-Stuffed Chicken, **74**
Southwestern Chili, **31**
Steak Chinois, **75**
Strawberry Banana Smoothies, **21**

T
Tortilla Chili Pie, **77**